HERESY AND REFORMATION IN THE SOUTH-EAST OF ENGLAND, 1520-1559

John F. Davis

D0126112

LONDON: Royal Historical Society
NEW JERSEY: Humanities Press Inc.
1983

BR 375
·D35
1983.

© John F. Davis 1983
Swift Printers Ltd ISBN: 0 901050 89 X
Humanities Press ISBN: 0 391 02874 X
All rights reserved

The Society records its gratitude to the following,
whose generosity made possible the initiation of
this series: The British Academy; The Pilgrim
Trust; The Twenty-Seven Foundation; The
United States Embassy Bicentennial Funds;
The Wolfson Trust; several private donors.

British Library Cataloguing in Publication Data

Davis, John F.
Heresy and reformation in the south-east of England,
1520 – 1559.
(Royal Historical Society studies in history series; no. 34).
1. Reformation – England
I. Title   II.   Series
274.2'06   BR375. D35   1983

1.   Reformation -England
2.   Heresies, Christian — England - History - 16th century
3   England - Church history - 16th century.

First published in Great Britain in 1983 by Swift Printers (Publishing) Ltd, London EC1
for The Royal Historical Society
and in the U.S.A. by Humanities Press Inc., Atlantic Highlands, NJ 07716

Printed in England by Swift Printers Ltd, London EC1

PREFACE

I dedicate this book to my parents, G.F. Davis and I.L. Travers, without whose material help it would have been impossible. I should like to thank my teachers and mentors who have helped me in the past: Miss Margaret Archer, who first introduced me to the delights of ecclesiastical records; Rev. Dr. T.M. Parker, my supervisor at Oxford; Professor A.G. Dickens who has always proffered help and advice; and latterly, Professor G.R. Elton, without whose enthusiasm this book would not have materialized. It remains for me to thank the staffs of all those libraries and record offices who have helped me through the course of my researches.

CONTENTS

ABBREVIATIONS

B.L.	British Library
B.S.H.P.F.	*Bulletin de la Société de l'Histoire Protestantisme Français*
C.C.L.	Canterbury Cathedral Library
C.U.L.	Cambridge University Library
E.S.R.O.	East Suffolk Record Office
G.L.	Guildhall Library
G.L.R.O.	Greater London Record Office
K.R.O.	Kent Record Office
L. & P.	*Letters and Papers, Foreign and Domestic, of Henry VIII*, ed. J.S. Brewer, J. Gairdner, R.H. Brodie (1862-1932)
L.P.L.	Lambeth Palace Library
N.N.R.O.	Norfolk and Norwich Record Office
P.R.O.	Public Record Office
R.D.R.	Rochester Diocesan Registry
W.S.R.O.	West Suffolk Record Office

1

THE MEDIEVAL CONTEXT:
THE CONTINUITY AND SURVIVAL OF LOLLARDY

It is now clear that Lollardy survived from its medieval beginnings in fairly robust form. References to Wyclif persist in Lollard trials. The heresiarch was praised, or thought to be a saint, or preferred to the fathers of the Church, in the years 1406, 1425, 1433, 1494, and 1518. His books were quoted as the source of heretical views in 1420-31, 1438, and 1520-12.[1] Owing to an efficient inquisition most of Wyclif's works now survive only in Prague, though a few English manuscripts are to be found one of which was entered into the treasurer's accounts of Oriel College, Oxford in 1454.[2] Some of Wyclif's postils on the books of Scripture were copied in Oxford in 1403 and came into the possession of the abbey of St Edmundsbury. Displaying marginalia in hands of the fifteenth and sixteenth centuries, they represent a possible source of inspiration to those reformers who were to originate from the same abbey.[3] While reform in the sixteenth century cannot be regarded as merely a revival of Lollardy it remains true that the movement owed a lot to the older heresy. It will be necessary to assume that ideas, like seeds, can hang suspended in the air, or lie dormant under the ground, until germinated by new and active minds. Wyclif's Latin works continued to circulate, while academic debate in Oxford, Cambridge and Paris at times recalled his controversial figure in its choice of theme, such as pilgrimages and the veneration of images.[4] The most read Latin manuscript of Wyclif's was the *De Trinitate* which contained useful material for the ordinary student of the schools while still bearing the seeds of controversial ideas.[5]

If we move away from the academic groves of abbey and university to the native traditions of later Lollardy, the evidence

---

[1] J.A.F. Thomson, *The Later Lollards, 1414-1520* (1965), 24, 29, 113, 130, 156, 162, 171, 179.

[2] L. Minio-Paluello, 'Two Erasures in MS. Oriel College 15', *Bodleian Library Record*, iv (1952-53), 207.

[3] B. Smalley, 'John Wyclif's *Postilla super totam Bibliam*', ibid., 188.

[4] Thomson, op. cit., 218-19; J. Crompton, 'Images and Pilgrimages Controversy', Oxford B. Litt. thesis (1950).

[5] A. du Pont Breck, 'The Manuscripts of John Wyclif's *De Trinitate*', *Medievalia et Humanistica*, vii (1952), 58, 68, 69.

becomes much clearer. Here we find definite localities preserving well marked traditions of belief. Lollardy was a gathered church with a number of divergent parties. At least three can be recognized. One was close to Wyclif's own beliefs, having a sacramentarian view of the eucharist; a second called in question all the seven sacraments of the Church; the third was antinomian and rationalistic. In 1520 there were three localities in the south-east with well developed traditions of Lollard belief. First, a broad corridor of northern Essex running from Colchester inland to Thaxted and extending from the Essex and Suffolk border of the Stour Valley to the textile villages of central Essex, such as Witham and Coggeshall. The second in importance lay in that part of the Kentish Weald which stretched to the north of the Kent and Sussex border between Rye and Hawkhurst. Major persecutions in both the fifteenth and sixteenth centuries unearthed Lollards here, specifically in the villages of Cranbrook, Tenterden, Benenden, Wittersham, Rolvenden, High Halden and Staplehurst. The third locality is to be found to the north-west of the metropolis, namely the wards of Coleman Street, Cripplegate, Cordwainer and Cheap.

All three areas were major textile producing centres, with a relatively high density of population and firm trading links. Literate craftsmen such as these had a more independent stance towards society and Church than did labourers. The rounds of middlemen and the dispatch to the ports of finished cloth provided routes for the circulation of both books and ideas. Lollard survival and the reception of continental reforming literature clearly owed much to this socio-economic organization. The textile artisan could migrate with greater freedom than the labourer, infecting other districts with heresy if he was a convinced Lollard, such as William Bull the Yorkshire shearman who returned to his native Dewsbury primed with new ideas of radical heresy which he had picked up in Hadleigh and other places in East Anglia.[6] In the London connection were to be found the craft halls and wool marts. The coastal traffic in wool also confirms the link between the traditions and the woollen industry, the ports of London, Colchester, Norwich, Rye and King's Lynn being in close proximity to heretical groups in the sixteenth century.

As more evidence comes to light, it appears that English Protestantism first flowered in areas having heterodox traditions. In the eighteenth century the Revd. John Lewis collected material for his *Brief History of the English Anabaptists* which included evidence of

---

[6] A.G. Dickens, *Lollards and Protestants in the Diocese of York, 1509-1558* (1959), 48.

the Kentish and Norfolk sects, finding 'the Religion of the Protestants no Novelty'.[7] Dr. Collinson has noted the Lollard antecedents underlying centres of Elizabethan Puritanism; the textile villages of the Stour Valley that sustained the Dedham Conference, and Cranbrook, the home of William Carder the weaver who had been the most important heretic of Archbishop Warham's persecution in 1511.[8] In addition the Puritan leaders in London held cures in the part of the metropolis where the old Lollard conventicles had flourished, in particular St. Giles Cripplegate and All Hallows Honey Lane.[9] Similarly, Dr. Thomson has summed up the legacy of later Lollardy as anti-sacerdotalism, anticlericalism, anti-papalism and puritanism.[10]

The diocese of Rochester had a Lollard tradition along the valley of the Medway. Evidence of conventicles arises at West Malling in 1425, at Hadlow in 1431, and at Tonbridge in 1496 where Christopher Payn confessed that he had been a Lollard for five or six years during which time he had held meetings in his house for the discussion of books. These books contained doctrines of an extreme kind: that there is no purgatory except in this world, that priests have no power to consecrate Christ's body, and that 'all the werkis of holy church be nought'.[11] A number of Rochester cases are of an antinomian character, suggesting continental influence, such as the Free Spirit heresy. On 9 October 1431 Thomas Hellis of Brenchley abjured articles such as that a priest in sin may not consecrate the elements, that however much a man persists in sin he shall not be damned, that adultery is no sin but a private transaction and a common solace, and that men and women are hypocrites when they perform their devotions in public. In particular, women who fast before the Holy Nativity and Pentecost, and receive absolution and communion, are to be 'rebukyd as evylleverys and to be withdrawe fro the devocion and luve of god'. In 1505 John Moress weaver of Rochester abjured similar heresies attacking Christ's passion and the person of the Virgin.[12] The continuity of certain complexions of heresy within the traditions can be instanced in the case of Kent. In 1428 the curate William Whyte of Tenterden fled with some of his followers to the

[7]Bodleian Library, MS. Rawlinson C 411, fo. 130r.

[8]P. Collinson, *The Elizabethan Puritan Movement* (1967), 96, 222.

[9]Ibid., 84-6.

[10]Thomson, op. cit., 251-3.

[11]R.D.R., Rochester Registers iii, Register Young, fos. 31v, 93v; iv, Register Savage, fo. 16v.

[12]Ibid., iii, fo. 93v.

Waveney Valley in Norfolk. Norfolk and Kentish heretics were caught up, however, in a persecution by Bishop Alnwick from 1428 to 1431. The outstanding feature of these trials was the extreme sacramentarian views of the accused, all seven sacraments being called into question. The lesser Norfolk tradition shows some continuity into the sixteenth century, but the outstandingly sacramentarian nature of the Kentish heretics is again manifest in Archbishop Warham's persecution in the Wealden villages in 1511.[13] By contrast, the London and Essex traditions show a consistent adherence to a more Wycliffite and evangelical belief. Another feature of Kentish extremism is to be found in Dutch influence when in 1511 one Simon Piers of Waldershare abjured an unorthodox Christology which implied that Christ took no flesh of the Virgin, a view which prefigures the Anabaptist doctrine of the celestial flesh.[14]

Yet another feature of the trials of 1511 is rampant anticlericalism. The most notorious case of an anticlerical riot occurred at Kennington where Richard Rickard kept the parish in a state of chaos. One of his cronies spoke against preachers and threatened to roast meat with the images of the saints, since their wood was the same as any other.[15] A parishioner of Milton maintained that he was as 'well occupied whan he is aboute his tubbis as the vicar whan he is at masse'. At Rolvenden, another parishioner chided his wife for believing the parson's assertion that every pilgrim's step towards a shrine brought pardon nearer, while he refused to believe in a reported miracle that a silk covering over some relics remained untouched when fire swept the parish church. He put down such talk as a means to dip into men's pockets.[16]

On the continent there is evidence of formal links between the old Waldensian church and the reformers. The Vaudois of Piedmont accepted reforming doctrines at Chanforan in 1532. Although Lollardy had some primitive organization in the shape of the Christian Brethren and the 'known men' or 'marked men', it failed to develop the sort of identity found among the Waldensians. These had a structured hierarchy, a seminary and library, and a network of colporteurs in France and Calabria.[17] The journeys of the barbs to visit the Rhenish reformers led to fraternal discussions on such subjects as pre-

[13] Thomson, op. cit., 125-132.

[14] L.P.L., Register Warham iii, fos. 175r-175v.

[15] Ibid., i, fo. 53v.

[16] Ibid., i, fo. 54r.

[17] E. Jalla, 'Farel et Les Vaudois de Piémont', in *Guillaume Farel* (1930) 286-7.

destination, and nicodemism.[18] Visits were also made to Bohemia to consult with the Unity of Brethren, and the united efforts of Waldensians and reformers resulted in a French bible.[19] There were other unions in Eastern Europe, but nothing of this kind occurred in England. In 1527, Two Lollards of Steeple Bumpstead met with Robert Barnes, and the result was far from happy. The reformer dismissed the Lollard books, 'a poynt for them', but succeeded in selling the visitors a Tyndale testament, 'For it is of more cleyner Englishe'. While Mrs Aston finds that it was part of the reformers' task to revive Lollard literature and put it in their polemical armoury, she also recognizes that a congruence of opinion on image worship, pilgrimage and clerical endowments must have brought the two movements together on a deeper level.[20] There was no straightforward move from pre-Reformation dissent into the post-Reformation Church, but the specific beliefs of the Lollard tradition were to play their part in shaping that Church's religion.

[18]E. Comba, 'L'introduction de la Réforme dans les vallées vaudoises du Piémont, 1530-1535', *B.S.H.P.F.*, xliii (1894), 11-12.

[19]G. Gonnet, 'Le premier Synode de Chanforan', ibid., xcix-c (1953-54), 217-19.

[20]M. Aston, 'Lollardy and the Reformation: Survival or Revival?', *History*, xlix (1964), 161, 166, 170.

2

PROCEDURES, COURTS AND RECORDS

Traditionally, heresy was exclusively the concern of the Church courts, and with the coming and going of various regimes between 1520 and 1559, these became sensitive to every changing wind. From 1520 to 1533 the courts maintained a heavy discipline upon the laity, with their supervision of morals, enforcement of Roman canonical religion, and the regulation of conduct touching such things as fasts and ceremonies. Heresy was a special case since it could be tried only before ordinaries – that is, bishops and inquisitors. The English Church occupied a position that was unique in Europe: the inquisition was excluded and torture banned. According to local custom those diocesan officials whose commission was 'generaliter', covering the whole diocese, could be regarded as ordinaries.[1] In the 1490s heresy was included in the jurisdiction of these officials for the first time, and the result was an increase in heresy trials.[2]

Heresy trials began with charging the accused with suspicion of heresy, and continued with the extortion of a confession. If, despite interrogation and the testimony of witnesses, the accused refused to confess, he was duly convicted, sentenced, and handed over to the secular authorities to be burnt. Trials usually ended in the abjuration of the accused, either at the stage of suspicion or at conviction. Relapse was thought to have taken place only if the accused confessed twice at the latter stage.[3] After abjuration followed penance, with the penitent standing bare footed and with head uncovered, bearing the emblem of the faggot of reeds. The articles of heresy were rehearsed during a public sermon, sometimes at the cathedral church as well as at the local church. Some act of penance was usually required during the public spectacle, such as the offering of a candle to the altar. There then followed a period of imprisonment or if the offence was less serious, the penitent was enjoined to fast or to make a donation to some charity. As well as the spiritual penalties the penitent could incur social stigma, as in the case of John Hig of Cheshunt who petitioned his bishop for the removal of the embroidered faggot since no one would employ him with it on.[4]

[1] W. Lyndwood, *Provinciale* (1967), 16, 18, 297.

[2] R.D.R., Rochester Registers, iv, Register Savage, fo. 2v.

[3] Lyndwood, *Provinciale,* 296, 305

[4] *L. & P.,* iv (ii), 4038(3).

Up to 1533 the ordinaries had the help of the secular arm at every turn. The medieval statutes for the suppression of heresy came into operation when Lollardy became revolutionary. Writs could be filed for the arrest and execution of heretics. The Statute of 1414 required all royal officials, from the chancellor down to mayors, to take an oath to eradicate heresy, while justices were to hold commissions of inquiry.[5] The reception of Lutheranism and Erasmianism prompted a royal directive of 20 October 1521 that all royal officers aid the bishop of Lincoln in the prosecution of heretics.[6] The court most used in major drives against Lollardy was the court of audience. Unlike the consistory court, which was presided over by the official principal or commissary general and tended to meet in a fixed venue, the court of audience was a peripatetic tribunal usually headed by the bishop himself.

Before going on to describe the anticlerical attack of 1533 upon the *ex officio* procedure against heresy, it will be worth noticing the mundane cases arising from the church courts that could lead to charges of heresy. A good deal of nonconformity occurred, while cases of defamation brought by the clergy against laymen mark the growth of anticlericalism. A 1522 libel case in London shows that the plaintiff had been defamed by a neighbour; 'And thou art an heretyke for thow tokyst not thy Ryghts at ester.'[7] Failure to comply with the Church's compulsory observances at Easter could bring the charge of heresy. William Smith, a butcher of Gravesend, was labelled a Lollard for having failed to keep the lenten fast of 1526. He had also neglected to communicate. Smyth's excuse that he had no money for his oblation was dismissed by Bishop Fisher as frivolous. After a spell of imprisonment Smith performed penance in his parish church and was enjoined to fast on bread and water at Whitsun.[8] A more obscure case from Ryarsh in 1522 tells how a parishioner had failed to observe the Easter customs because he and the vicar 'wer att debate for the giffyng of the holy loff'. The accused had actually been advised by an acquaintance to leave the district.[9]

Failure to attend the confessional could be due to a lack of integrity on the priest's part. Another Kentish case of 1524 tells how parishioners at Pembury accused their vicar of making the miller's

[5] 2 H.V. cap. 7, *Statutes of the Realm* (1810-28), II, 125-128.

[6] D. Wilkins, *Concilia* (1737), III, 698.

[7] G.L.R.O. Deposition Book, DL/C/207, fo. 10r.

[8] K.R.O., Rochester Act Book, DRb/Pd/8, fo. 120r.

[9] ibid., fo. 77r.

confession public. One parishioner was led to comment that it was preferable to be shriven by the lions at the Tower of London than by the vicar.[10] A couple of London cases from the same period illustrate how clerical exactitude could result in trouble. One parishioner had been refused communion because he had openly declined to live in charity with his neighbours. Another failed to make the Easter confessional and could not produce a certificate that showed he had done so elsewhere. The vicar charged the offender to search his conscience, only to be told that his conscience was as good as the priest's.[11] Perhaps the most common offence was absenteeism. Many people found work preferable to worship, the sort of occupations which could keep the faithful from their duty being fishing, milling, and the selling of books in St. Paul's churchyard.[12] Yet another offender was Robert Bewte who denied that he had advised his neighbours to watch their sheep rather than attend at a visitation. More secular concern was behind the opinion of Lollards who, appearing before Bishop Grey of Ely, asserted that labourers should be exempt from fasting.[13]

The high level of abuses in the Church gave rise to further misgivings in the period 1520 to 1533. An earlier case sets the scene. Richard Gavell abjured opinions before Bishop Fisher that included criticism of the local clerical life style: 'Now the prest standeth in the pulpet and he doth no thyng but chide and brawell For I loke more on his lief than of his wordes whare so ever he saith there'.[14] A similar opinion was voiced in 1523 by Joanna Gurner of Ashford; 'I am ass goode a woman as thou art a preste'. On 18 January 1527 Alice Feharry was cited in a case of defamation for calling the prior of Rochester names; 'A vengaunce and a muscheff on hym horson hokid nose scott'. James Philcocke of the same diocese also roundly condemned the morals of another priest: 'an unthrifty a lecherows & a bowdy pryst and a nowghty levyer of his body'.[15] Any fracas in church brought with it the danger of pollution by effusion of blood. On 14 May 1520 a case came before the vicar general of London in which one Browne had brawled with a 'knave priest', resulting in a blood-letting in church – 'half spoonfull blode'.[16] Most of these cases ended

[10]ibid., fos. 32r, 32v.

[11]G.L.R.O., Vicar General's Book, DL/C/330, fo. 75v.

[12]K.R.O., DRb/Pd/7, fos. 36v, 37v: G.L.R.O., DL/C/3, fo. 3r.

[13]Historical MSS. Commissioners, 12th. Report, Appendix iv (1891), 384

[14]R.D.R., Rochester Registers iv, Register Fisher, fo. 47r.

[15]K.R.O., DRb/Pd/7 fo. 234r: DRB/Pd/8 fo. 32v:DRb/Pd/9 fo. 53r.

[16]G.L.R.O., DL/C/330, fo. 8r.

with a submission by the offender as in the case of Joanna Gurner: 'I am sory that I have said a myss to my curate'. Some affrays were of a purely domestic character. In 1530 a holy water clerk of Wouldham had punched a chorister on the nose strictly in the line of duty, 'holde thy pease boye & synge rigth'.[17]

It is unlikely that churchmen held heresy trials out of pure malice. What they required was a confession of heretical opinions that were sincerely held. They were very jealous over their jurisdiction, however, and threats of hauling the laity up on heresy charges could be made. In a letter of 1515 Bishop Nix of Norwich directed the bailiffs of Ipswich to beware of their townspeople who were seeking to limit episcopal absolution: 'verely whosoever holdyth suche oppinions he savorithe of heresy.'[18]

For the *ex officio* procedure to function effectively formularies of articles used in interrogation had to be sensitive to current heretical opinion. In the period 1520 to 1533 came the reception of Lutheranism, and very soon the whole deluge of reforming ideas burst upon the scene in the shape of imported books from the continent. In these years the bishops spent a lot of energy in bringing their lists of articles of suspected heresy up to date. In 1521 Wolsey sent out mandates to all bishops to deal with Lutheran literature and the heresies they contained. One of the list of forty-two errors of the new heresy tersely expressed solifidianism: 'Haec sola fides facit eos puros et dignos'.[19] A similar list that Wolsey used against a suspect in 1529 contained a discordant note: 'That the body of Christ is not in the sacrament but only bread and wine'.[20] Since this sacramentarian article would have been treated as heresy by Lutheran and Catholic alike, its inclusion on the list suggests that Wolsey was aware that he was dealing with mixed heresy of some sort. Another possibility is that academics were suspected of Lutheranism, while the artisan was still regarded as the most likely kind of Lollard. This is probably behind the two opposing sets of interrogatories used in the major trial of Thomas Bylney and Thomas Arthur, leaders of reform at Cambridge. One, a Lutheran list in Latin, was used, another in English, entered in the margin of the register, was not used. The English articles were Lollard in tone: 'Is it not an heresie to beleve that the very fleshe and blode of crist is not in

[17] ibid., DL/C/207, fo. 147r.

[18] E.S.R.O., Depositions, A. v.12, fo. 220r.

[19] Wilkins, *Concilia*, III, 690-3.

[20] *L.&P.*, iv, ii, 4444 (i).

the sacrament of thautre and or that the very bred and wyne remayneth after the consecration.'[21]

In view of the circulation of heretical books at the universities the judges assumed that they were dealing with Lutherans rather than with Lollards. That such a distinction was made elsewhere in Europe is shown by the practice of imperial judges in Franche-Comté where Lutherans were left to the secular *parlements* and Waldensians to the Inquisition.[22]

Turning to the books that were creating so much apprehension on the part of the bishops, a list published on 24 May 1530 articled the heresies that had been found by a board of investigators under the chairmanship of Archbishop Warham and including the more pliant Cambridge reformers Edward Crome and Hugh Latimer. The first two books were by William Tyndale and were considered the most likely to corrupt the people. These were *The Wicked Mammon* and *The Obedience of a Christian Man*, books breathing a spirit of popular Lutheranism, 'Feith oonly doth justifie us'. Other doctrines from the books included the putting to doubt of free will and good works, the priesthood of all believers, the doctrine of the calling, that purgatory was a papal invention, and that papal authority concerned preaching and nothing else. The next book to be dissected, *The Revelation of Anticriste* by John Frith, contained similar heresy but enjoined a more explicit biblicism, 'that nothinge shulde be doon, but that which is expresly rehersed in Scripture'. Besides this extremism, it attacked universities and scholasticism, and held that John Hus had been condemned for believing the word of God. *The Sum of Scripture* was a yet more leftish work that had been translated by Simon Fish and contained Rhenish influences that owed as much to Erasmus as Luther. The typical Erasmian ethic comes to the fore in the assertions that Christians should not indulge in law suits or warfare. The same author's work, *The Book of Beggars*, was well known for its attack on purgatory, while the chief error found in Joye's *Prymer* was his omission of the saints and our Lady. The last work, a translation by Roye of a Lutheran exposition of I Corinthians VII, was mainly a condemnation of monasticism and the vow of chastity.[23]

The bishops' plans to eradicate the new and the old heresies were not only ill-conceived but were brought to a halt by the growing storm of anticlericalism in the years 1529 to 1533. Books were burnt and the

[21] G.L., Register Tunstall, 9531/10, fos. 132v-133v.

[22] L. Febvre, *Notes et Documents sur la Réforme et L'Inquisition en Franche-Comté* (1912), 31.

[23] Wilkins, *Concilia*, III, 727-8.

trial of both Lollards and reformers went ahead but with increasing difficulty. Thomas More, the champion of the old Church, not only took on the task of combating heresy as chancellor but succeeded too well for the liking of the king. As the breach with Rome developed, Henry could find anti-papal reformers a welcome innovation. The laity began to find the bishops' *ex officio* heresy proceedings more and more obnoxious. In successive drafts of the 'Supplication against the Ordinaries' specific complaints were made; that innocent men were cited for heresy out of malice; that innocent men were accused without the supporting evidence of reliable witnesses; that men were trapped by subtle and unfair interrogation; that the evidence of reliable witnesses favourable to the accused was not allowed into court; and that heresy trials were initiated against any who justly reproved the clergy for their evil lives.[24] It is likely that the two trials of Thomas Bylney had given rise to these grievances. The main feature of the first trial in 1527 was Bylney's refusal to answer to the articles of heresy brought against him. He claimed that in a preaching tour of East Anglia and London in the same year he had preached no heresy, and pleaded that he should be allowed to call witnesses to prove his innocence. After the testimony of witnesses called by the tribunal of judges, Bylney abjured but returned to his preaching in 1531 and suffered the penalty of relapse in Norwich. In the second trial he appealed to be heard before Henry himself, having heard that the king had assumed a new title.[25]

The impression that Bylney had public support is strengthened by the pains More went to in his *Dialogue concerning Tyndale* of 1528 to justify the treatment that Bylney had received. More undertook to combat certain current rumours concerning Bylney and the reformation in general. It was being said that false accusations had been made against Bylney, as they had been made against Luther himself: that honest priests in London considered that Bylney had been victimized because he had preached against abuses rife among friars and other clergy; and that Bylney was an honest man whose preaching edified the people. Further rumours concerned Tyndale's *New Testament* – that it had been burnt in order to hide the truth from the eyes of laymen who would otherwise see how far the clergy and the pope had sunk from the standards expected of them. Any who wished to read the scriptures in their mother tongue were regarded as Lutherans, while

[24]G.R. Elton, 'The Commons' Supplication of 1532: Parliamentary Manoeuvres in the Reign of Henry VIII', *E.H.R.,* lxvi (1951), 531, 521-532.

[25]E. Gow, 'Thomas Bylney and his relations with Sir Thomas More', *Norfolk and Norwich Archaeological Society,* xxxii (1958-61), 300.

any preacher who went in for plain speaking about abuses had his mouth shut by accusations of heresy. More sought to silence this criticism by stressing Bylney's manifest heresy that had been established by many witnesses – that no worship should be made to images, that no prayer should be offered to saints, and that pilgrimages were unprofitable.[26] The two beneficed clerks who wrote to the bishops claiming that Bylney was innocent turned out to be Forman and Garard, heretical book agents at both universities. Finally, More dismissed Bylney's excuse that he could not remember what he had preached since he had preached so often.[27]

It is likely that More came to hear about these rumours through his close association with the London diocesan officials. The vicar-general of London dealt with a small number of cases in which similar criticism had been made. In 1525 a preacher at St Paul's Cross had repeated some hearsay to the effect that some were neglecting their devotions and refusing to light candles before images: 'And they say that if lutheris bookys were not [sic] brent they wold be contented to be brent with them'. Offensive words uttered by two parishioners of St Andrew's Eastcheap echoed *the Dialogue* in 1527. John Parkyns was accused of saying: yf I had xx bokes of the holye scriptor translatyd in to Englishe I wold bringe noon of them in for my lord of london, curse he or blesse he for he dothe it bycause we shuld have no knowlege but kepys it all secrete to hym self. William Jonson was brought to book for having praised Luther's works, and for saying that if he had his way they would be published throughout the realm. Finally, a priest of St Andrew Undershaft denied uttering a defence of Bylney: 'my lord of london will suffre no man to preche at powles crosse but flaterers and dissemblers for they that say treuth er ponyshed as bylney and Arthure was.'[28]

The result of all this rumour, criticism and the drift away from Rome appeared in 1533 when the secular law (the act of 25 Henry VIII c.14) profoundly altered procedure in heresy cases. Trials could now be initiated only after an indictment at common law, or by the accusation of two witnesses. The very meaning of heresy had been changed, as when Henry intervened in the trial of Edward Crome, declaring that an article of the accused that denied papal supremacy should be struck out since 'it was quite certain and true'.[29] So long as

---

[26] Thomas More, *Dialogue concerning Tyndale,* ed. Campbell (1931), 6-13.

[27] ibid., 176-197.

[28] G.L.R.O., DL/C/330, fos. 100r, 137v, 138v, 164r.

[29] *L.&.P.,* v, 148.

witnesses were called, however, the consistory courts could function more or less as before. The bishops had to be more careful since royal writs hedged the procedure of heresy trials around. The imperial ambassador speculated that Bishop Nix's imprisonment for praemunire resulted from his burning of Thomas Bylney without the king's writ.[30] On 4 February 1533 Thomas Phillip, a leading light of the Lollards who had obstructed the *ex officio* procedure, petitioned the Commons and sought a writ of wrongful arrest.[31] Some took a wider meaning from the act of 1533, that ordinaries could not now sit as judge over heretics unless empowered to do so by a royal commission. Moreover, if the bishop's case proved inadequate to establish guilt, then a writ of wrongful imprisonment might be obtained. Or again, if the king showed an interest in the trial, a royal pardon might be granted.[32]

An undated letter from Bishop Stokesley to the lord Chancellor illustrates the degree of lay control that now existed. John Faley, parish clerk of St Peter's Colchester, had been indicted with four others. The four stood trial and were dismissed; 'that other iiii answerid before me and after that I had thoroughly examined them I sent their answers and confessions to my lorde Chauncellor accordeng to his request and accordeng to their desertes and his mynde and pleasor despached them.' Faley on the other hand refused to answer to anyone but the chancellor himself. He had already abjured once and now stood condemned of a Lutheran article on confession. After some delay he submitted and was released on sureties. Another who appeared at the same time, John Coole, was a more serious case, having been indicted of sacramentarian heresy before many witnesses. He appealed to be heard by the king himself, and he was duly sent to the chancellor with his indictment.[33]

However, the clergy were not content to let the prosecution of heresy drift wholly into lay control. On 23 June 1536, the lower house of Convocation produced a list of current heresy known as the *mala dogmata*. The first of these sixty-seven errors left no doubt as to the kind of heresy it meant: 'why should I see the sacring of the high mass? is it any thing else but a piece of bread or a little pretty round Robin'. Of those articles that can be positively identified, thirty-seven are characteristic of Lollardy while seventeen are couched in terms of popular solifidianism and biblicism similar to the earlier list extracted

[30]ibid., vii, 171.
[31]ibid., vii, 155.
[32]B.L., Cotton Cleopatra, F. ii, fos. 250r, 251r.
[33]ibid., E. V, fos. 410-410v.

Other volumes in this series

Copies obtainable on order from
Swift Printers Ltd, 1-7 Albion Place, Britton Street, London EC1M 5RE

274.206
DAV

BR375
·D35
1983

Davis, John F.

HERESY AND REFORMAT
East of england, 152

	DATE DUE	

Kansas School of Religion
At the University of Kansas
Smith Hall, Rm. 109, Library
Lawrence, Kansas 66045-2164